# LANTSKIP

Paradise Lost and the Classical Epic, 1979

The Motive for Metaphor: Essays on Modern Poetry
in honor of Samuel French Morse (with Guy Rotella) 1983

Lantskip, 1987

# LANTSKIP

*by Francis Blessington*

1987

William L. Bauhan, Publisher
Dublin, New Hampshire

Library of Congress Cataloging-in-Publication Data
Blessington, Francis C., 1942-
Lantskip.
I. Title
Ps3552.L443L3     1987     811'.54     87-1116
ISBN 0-87233-090-7

Published 1987 by William L. Bauhan, Publisher
Old County Road, Dublin, N.H. 03444

Printed in the United States of America

*To My Mother*

# Acknowledgments

Some of these poems appeared in *Argo, Ariel, Arizona Quarterly, The Classical Bulletin, Cumberland Poetry Review, Denver Quarterly, Descant, Gargoyle, Harvard Magazine, Italian Quarterly, Lucky Star, New Collage Magazine, Off Main Street, Riverside Quarterly, Soundings East, Southern Humanities Review, Stone Country, The Thoreau Journal Quarterly, Yale Literary Magazine.*

# Contents

# LANTSKIP

I

# First Deer Hunt, First Poem

Everything caused it: my being the boy
who had to drive his stunned deer
across the half-frozen pond, the coy
rest and throttling hoof clatter

away on more breaking ice,
the crash again through thin crust,
till it slid against the steeper shore face.
I had flushed a doe from the stiff forest.

But now, winged, the struggle was its own.
The legs bracketed the footless ice below,
trying, trying to mount, but hunking down,
exhausted on the floe, like a sea cow.

It couldn't work, so I had to axe
wedges. There the water gushed.
Not even the pond lined such straight tracks.
Then I scared the deer up into the brush.

# Cow Skull

There was no special
Neglect in it: roads,
Two caves, the smash
Above the nose bridge
To tell you ants
Didn't do that. Resting
On a greenless field
Stolen from O'Keeffe.

Still kids, we mounted
It before the cottage.
Slid the outer horn
Off and left honeycomb
Pricked for attention.

It grew on grass
All high summer.
Then swelled the horizon:
Noseless, horned mountains,
The yard its lower jaw.

## *Sons*

Filled with whiskey or love,
my grandfather kneels
in the dark of the church. He prays
boldly, fearfully aloud.
He talks only to God,
and digs the foundations of streets.

My father, a boy, brings
pork sandwiches to the edge
of the ditch. His eyes divert.
They follow the old man's
past the pick, hooked
in the canal like an anchor.

Down the scooped silence,
grandfather will pound
the macadam so built-to-last
my father scans the ridgepoles
of jumbled houses, turreted,
and belted with verandahs.

He sees himself perched
above roads not needing repair.
He hears the chatter of families.
He sees his father crane
at his hammer, raised like a monstrance
above the congregation.

A boy, I drag shingles
to the roof. My father's eyes
wander first now.
From the shoulders of houses, we
pry into the dark
of the light-blue silences.

# Ridge

Beneath the quibbling bare trees
rags of snow
needles and sunburnt oak leaves
the stiffening wind
and winter still behind the Rockies.
For Emerson
a quartz slab perfecting sundown.
Short stones
white like teeth for Thoreau and Hawthorne
pitted and shimmed
on the esker's even outcropped edge
itself a tomb
humped north to the clear pond.
On his ledge
in November cleanness, Ellery Channing
wielding
his obscured black slate tablet
on the evening
like one last chastening blanket.

# Quabbin

You can never be lost here, or ground sold.
The clouds swallow sun, grow October chill.
Old field stones, naked, spider-filled,
run through potted woods nowhere. Fooled
you skirt the hem of a pond, clumsy alders
shoved in water, steep with collapsing snow.
Deer prints padding the thicketed farms know
better the marked, stunted watercourses.
You crash fat oak leaves free of frost,
bee-lining the last sunset hour, past
the sacrifice of a Ford, blackened
steel charred to nitrate. The mechanism
which paints ground and pitch pine blood-rust
fills owl-light with what it has to do.

# Christmas Card

A tall woodpecker rattles his ghost song
boldly against December's moonlit sun.
He preaches tardy red-tooth maple sugar
lessons of early wintering October,
then flourishes a branch of fir, to test
resistance to the laminated frost.
His swinging must broadcast the smell of fir
which warms nostalgic as a cobbled fire.
It pools up the bare wood, as from a kettle,
then steams slow, trucked through towns, later to settle
on writers who nod in their whiskey sleep,
and dream the woods to dark marks on white sheets.

Beneath that fir, what must be half-imagined
unless dug out, the Christmas fern. Wind-tanned
to age on top, it drives in snow its green—
secretive, deep, whole, live, and undefined—
the winter wheat of these New England farms.
It spins its circle like dune grass on sand.
We watch it grip, inspired to rebel,
silent, almost, against the winter's will.
It makes of snow the form to mold its speech
when the full nights browse down the sun's last week.
Its plastic leaf binds spring in new half-life,
to share with us some part of weather's insight,
to show this plant reclaim the northern forest
and speak to you in words of wilderness,
and speak to you, in words, our Merry Christmas.

# Dogtown (1719–1830)[1]



"Dogtown is delusion."
Joseph E. Garland, *The Gloucester Guide.*

Though winter now, the year still promises.
The wind drags west full nets of salt and mist
above the thinning ice of a false sea,
where past springs rummage through the parted rocks.
Here land is high, the topsoil sparse for farms,
since ice dropped in fat cannonades of stones.

No gulls bother to pick the trash, so stones
and sand lie stacked with boxtop promises.
A cache of barberries still harrows farms
which failed when granite could not sink the mist
but wrinkled crevices for swamps. The rocks
stay stuck in sky, uncleared by ox or sea.

Where fog heaves in its sodden bales of sea
blue aster and sweet fern once burst through stones,
and barns and booths were shadowed in the rocks,
as if a witch had painted promises
to interest them in clinkers, salt and mist,
who cut the common land for parcelled farms.

Potato pits and cellar holes held farms
when hazel trees stopped waving flags at sea.
Around the oval square in frequent mist,

[1]An abandoned settlement on the coast of Gloucester,
Massachusetts. Feral dogs once gathered there.

some wishbone bonnets prayed, but on the stones
"Aunt" Rachel's coffee grounds made promises
and sold her "springish" drink beneath the rocks.

Then roads revolted, left the town to rocks.
Five years is all it takes to sink all farms.
Widows hoarded their seamen's promises,
stone walls divorced and fell down toward the sea.
From feral dogs too wild above the stones
the daffy crouched in barrows of gray mist.

Now cellar holes boast numbers in that mist.
KINDNESS, WORK, and TRUTH are carved on the rocks.
We feel the glacial slip and drag of stones.
It bolsters pride of craft in other farms
to pass by there beside the barking sea
that leaps for visitors in promises.

Today in mist, we target-shoot the farms.
Echoed on rocks, the bullets dull to sea
like stones, in natural cairns of promises.

## Tenants Harbor

In the middle of our way you complain:
night-fog and seaweed choke
the smooth-rolled hummock.

I gripe: is lichen so thick
it tricks spore to seed?
We wrangle in our dark net.

For Monhegan Island, a buoy
tongues its vowels like a seal.
Fills the ether with soliloquy.

Our talk tightens to telegram.
I recall spread on ocean
your face in your cold cream mask.

Resonant to islands, I shudder
for that morning's flagged bay:
the land falling in tide,

old-squaw swelled in circles,
the loose performance of gulls,
who hastened past in pairs.

# *Ad Patrem*

There's not much left now:
Tools tent cobwebs
In the cellar, the gold rust
Spills on the floor tracked by mice.

Shears hung like malefactors;
Nibbled extension cords; the tired
Slats that made foolish skis.
The wood bench spreads its bier beside the vise.

Sample the re-enforced barrels
With your foot, stir the dim poured motes,
Shake the shafts funnelled from windows.
It's summer now, and the furnace unsifted.

# Antiphon on Monomoy Island

What sounds in the salt gust? *Ghost.*
What unseen calculations for this morain? *More rain.*
What will become of this heeling island? *Land.*
And us hearing silt dent the seiner? *Saner.*
Why bring goldeneye to winter? *To inter.*
Why dune grass webs sand together? *To gather.*
What makes you so articulate? *You, late.*

II

# Ancestral Visit

Grandfather waved goodbye last
across the meadow from that gate,
but a century ago the whitewashed stone
was not a cow shed, and the school
did not roof a milk cart with iron.

These people never knew me:
the son slogs, cap and boots,
his declining mother spat
at a New York relation who refused
to step in the cow-flapped byre.

The crooked road leads finally out.
I feel still the wet of their kiss,
like water off these Leitrim marshes.
Where ground molds a miniature Switzerland,
drivers stop only for leavetakings.

## The Lisbon Poem

Before we descended to the waters of that city,
We drove by cork trees till there was no more west.
Where the river flattens and sails,
Guidebooks told us the bridges changed
   names with the revolutions,
And Jesus, like a huge cement chimney-pot,
Blesses the speech of the building cranes.
Prince Henry offers the toy model of a ship,
Praying in stone that the Renaissance come true.
On a hill above him is a garden of pomegranates.
In the sky clouds shunt like galleons.
We enter as if we had one city to go.

A rotten submarine bellies up
Its frozen carcass in the harbor,
And a statue grimaces on its knees.
We think back on atlases and are not sure.
No two clocks agree.
Why, we say, do we come?
Your face turns as sour as the Infante's in the portrait
Where Prince Henry glares his old face
At the innocence of Saint Vincent.
And Bosch's Temptation of Saint Anthony screams
From the museum like a gull.

It took us long to understand
How in a church, famous for Inquisition,
Beggars pray in a hulk of seared rubble.

How the macho laughter of cafes threshes
The polluted surf of the beach,
How a boy reads aloud the drunken poetry of Pessoa.
That language jogs our memory with the language of shells.

In white limestone inlaid with black basalt,
The street rolls and foams.
We have arrived at our destination, love,
Without knowing it—the endless western seas
That burnished Prince Henry's history,
The gravel that crunches like bone.
The ducks that rise, like flags.

# Dartmoor in Winter

FOR ANN

Fifty gulls each in its own green
Spill their whiteness.

And the wild horses
Who will gallop fitfully over the gorse in moonlight.

The cold rain
Fills me with the fifty foot tors

That rise in stone across the sea,
Across all Ireland.

The wetness rests,
And the fox who outran the foppish hunters.

With them we listen at night
To the windstorm.

In pub candlelight the sign
Swings over, over at its own sweet will.

And we feel
The horses fly unimpeded

Across the silver gorse.

# At the Grave of John Buchan

*At the Grave of John Buchan*

"Gang as if ye was something growing"—Gillie saying

The vicar half smiles, "Only his ashes."
A disc half-mystical and pseudo-Egyptian,
Usual cherishing prayers
About friends, *Nostrae Patriae*, the plowing muses.
Fetid nettles, staple for home-fashioned beer,
A sun-lid for senescent empires.


You would find me modern: "chronic" and underfed
So every year you bandied more works,
Casts from fly-books,
Cribbed tales, history to flout your toy Oxford,
Forced from the leisure of your sick child-bed year
To take long looks.


Rich grass scampers at this field's edge,
Barley bowing like your officious negroes, and the sun
Draws wheat to cane—
All miscast, as your wish for "buried in Africa."
Sky ruffles to confusing seas, cars
Thresh the loosened grain.


For you things connect: poison yews
Pen you, gunless, beneath a ventriloquizing quail.
In the lagged summer heat

They candle you at corners, the circle squared.
The wife outlasting another thirty years
Obedient at your feet.


Clover spreads like hands. I recroft and name
The plain below in your hobbledehoy rivers.
A layabout, I try to bless
The clear familiars of your left-off fishing book
And you, amidst all your errata, in dirt making
An earthy roundness.

# The Abandoned Monastery on Skellig Michael[1]

We come looking for what they wished to be,
to feel a fresh response from thrumming wind,
in rhythms of rain and fuchsia, stone and sea.

Mornings the monks intoned a chant like bees
then swarmed their boats. To hollow-hived *clocháns*
we come looking for what they wished to be.

Our saints ate puffins, full of fish, God's quarry:
can we dream ourselves puffins, driving home
in rhythms of rain and fuchsia, stone and sea?

Island preserve, a cocksure hermit's need,
tricks us from prophecy to revelation:
we come looking for what they wished to be:

blue weather and limed rock, the galed sea-puppy,
the mewing gulls or mizzling waves which swoon
in rhythms of rain and fuchsia, stone and sea.

The rock-cut runes read possibility:
did monks snap bladder campion at Danes?
We come looking for what they wished to be
in rhythms of rain and fuchsia, stone and sea.

[1]Off the Irish coast, destroyed by Danes.

# Kingfisher

Flicker of leaf,
shard of light,

transgresses the riverbank;
the bold smallness intimates
a noisome prehistoric glade,
where all chirps and flits
and hunts.

It was probably large and masterful,
as the pterodactyl,
and the pterodactyl feared it,
drawing heat from the same sun
in its high-arching jump,
warming the river salts,
snatching the seed.

Bold as a pygmy shrew,
he flickers,
and brings the willow silver.

Blue-green,
green-blue patches
harrow the squat river fish,

Color-spatterer,
the biological necessity
mans the portages,
delves the mud-gray days.

Self-sufficient
eater, creator,
in the deliberate cruise
of metal blue.

Sword-bill
haling the yellow air,
little fisher-king,
traverse and navigate the river wind.

Forerunner,
take me
with you in your determined leap,

chlorophyl flutter,
drop of green.

## *Mowing Italy*

Yellow leaped
above ground.
But no more.
Even snakes
honor vibes
of Home Rule,
dimensions
lost to close
green order.
I sprinkle
what sulphur
sky won't bleach.
Armies could
parade my
flattened earth
cleared of its
foreignness.

## The Iron Column of Meharauli[1]

Was pressed solid.
No rust or charring,
Though not the fault of climate,
Perhaps talent or the ground.

Like a thorn, it spindles
In the brutal light.
Its platform plays
A hod for earth.

The gonfalon
And the official prostitutes
Left it at the forced marches,
More poignant

Than braggart phallus.
Or the unciphered
Sanskrit victory
Niched on the heavenly tongue.

Undwarfed, it preens
Taller than childhood.
Around it, in back of you,
Brace arms for luck.

[1]Built in the fourth century A.D., this column stands near Delhi.

Circle yourself.
Blind again, your spine unbends.
At your feet, dust mingles.
And burns.

# Burning Ghat

Beyond the spice market,
the saffron, tumeric, and myrrh,
below The Golden Temple,
where walls weed out rickshaws,
I lose myself in aisles
of vermilion cottons,
burnished copper, and oranges,
and follow the veiled litters
to the posh odor of woodsmoke,
the crackling steps.

The stoking begun and the unstoking,
air closes to cave.
Yellow sheers to sky.
In the red soil
where the black flags glisten,
part of hearth and flood and spindrift,
I am home.

## Nairobi in Winter

In green climates you are never sure.
After midnight the bulbs burn weak.
Watchmen lean on their clubs. And sleep
Where air is mile-thin, but endures.

Under Jacaranda and Bougainvillaea,
Hyenas, unmolested, steal down
Through bought White Highland farms.
They light the dark with fetid hair.

Trucks humble the sharp plateau,
Battened on huts by broken shoulders,
Or northern tribes beheaded by the equator.
For days the same kites float.

Out west, the Masai brush the landscape.
Free, faint laughter stirs their red capes.

## Photographing the Love Birds
## of Masai Mara: A Pastoral

Under our rover's shade, we snap migrations
countless as Buffalo Bill's sniped from his train.
A lion fondles a zebra carcass, tanned to black.
She blends us downwind, another termite mound.
Vultures cluster like sable fruit.
Bands of wildebeest maneuver scabrous brush to pools.
Clumped thorn trees sprinkle fine hands
and bend their spears against big grass.
In the center, Masai men swing their oarlock ears,
tell of their diet of blood and milk.
Cool and circumcised, the women hover,
crumbs beneath the table land.
Animal spoor sweetens the lawn of Serengeti
and old green reshoots the fire-built barricade
to Tanzania. The snorting passage, the natural rift
camouflages again the tribal crawl.
Summer so swells the breed and give
of each beast for itself and others
it almost forgives our kills:
guiltless fever trees shade the lime of bones.
In Saint George's zeal, the zebra goes down,
makes birds more general and beyond catalogues.
The Yoruba sing, "When Ilbrahim is hungry, he eats a
    baboon."
—the flak of equatorial marriages and human loves.

# Caryatid Song

Carry the black sea
To the top of this hill.

Loose from my skull
The blind frieze.

Free from my feet
The dropped earth.

III

# Paolo and Francesca

Dante, *Inferno*

I

Doleful notes started and forced
Me to feel their lamentation.
Now groaning beat its course
In a place where all light is dumb,
That bellows like the sea, pressed
And warred against by repugnant winds.
The furious buffeting never rests
But goads the spirits with awesome rapture,
Turning and torturing in endless contest.
Near the ruin, the gutted fissure,
The souls scream, wail and lament.
There they curse the Eternal Power.
I knew that with such affliction,
They damn and punish the fleshly sinners
Who raise desire over reason.
As wings lift the starlings in winter
Months to a wide, full flock,
The shades are herded through air:
Down, up, here, there, they follow the shock.
No hope ever comforts them
Of rest, or even to be less racked.
As cranes fly chanting their anthems
And make in air one long line,
I watched them come, casting complaints,
The souls transported by that whirlwind.
"Master," I asked, "Who are these so
Whipped by this black wind?"

II

"The first sinner you would know
Was empress," he told me,
"She ruled many tongues, and knew
Her soul so broken in lechery
She made vice lawful in her laws,
To dye the shame she lives by.
She is Semiramis, I have read she was
Successor to Ninus and his wife,
Who held the lands the Sultan chastises.
That other, Dido, pyred herself:
She betrayed the ashes of Sichaeus.
There's Cleopatra, randy queen of Egypt,
And Helen, for her such tangled ruckus
Spun the years, and grand Achilles:
Love battled him down at last.

III

See Paris, Tristan. He pointed a million
Shades and more, gave names,
Those love severed from this life.
After I heard my master defame
Those ancient ladies and knights,
Pity yoked me. I was insane.
"Poet," I started, "Might
I call those two grafted together,
Who seem to lie on air so lightly?"
He to me, "You'll discover
When they draw near. Beg them by
The love that leads, and they must favor."

The wind heaves our side:
I cry, "Aggrieved souls, hear!
Come talk if no One denies."
Like doves lashed by desire
Who fly with uplifted wing, when they home
to the sweet nest, shot through air,
These drove from Dido's flock and ran
to us riding the fetid blackness.
So strong was my loving summons.

IV

"O living creature, courteous and gracious,
You condescend to visit this purple
Atmosphere and us, who colored the grass
With blood. If the Ruler of All People
Could hear, we would pray Him
To give you peace who pity our plight.
Whatever pleases you to speak or listen
We'll obey and tell you both.
Or listen to you while the wind weakens.
My birthplace lolls on the coast
Where the Po drops and shunts
To make with its tributaries a peace.
Love fires the gentle heart
and joined this man to my beauty, torn
From me with a suddenness that still haunts.
Love pardons no lover from loving in return
and pleasure binds with iron ties.
To my side, as you see, they have nailed him.
Love led us together to die.
Caina awaits who snuffed our life."

V

Such was the speech ferried
From these wounded souls. My face
Turned toward the earth and froze.
The poet asked, "What thoughts race
In your mind?" I groaned,
"What softness, what great desire steers
Sorrowing souls to this black home?"
I moved their way. I inquired,
"Francesca, your martyred lives
Make me weep, brimful of fear.
Tell me, in the season of candied sighs,
How did love reveal his sweetness,
How did you sense his dangerous drives?'

VI

And she to me, "No greater sadness
Than reliving joy in misery.
Your master knows that wretchedness.
But if to grasp the root of my
Love you have such deep-fed passion,
I'll tell you like some weeping story
Teller: that day we read for fun
Of Lancelot in love's stranglehold.
We were alone, beyond suspicion.
The romance made our eyes take hold.
Our faces whitened with the strain.
That spot alone conquered:
When the thirsty smile drained
The great lover's kiss. Then,

50

One forever soldered in my pain
Kissed this mouth all shaken—
The book is a pimp, and so is its author—
That day we never read again."

VII

One spirit played the tale-teller.
The other muttered. Dumb with compassion,
I fainted, shrunk to a spectre.
Then dropped—a corpse, a dead ruin.

# IV

## Vis Inertiae

The ice cap retreated—
Perceptibly—in time. The falling
Wall revealed itself uneternal.

From a tall latitude, you watched
Pure savanna. You had to step back.
Then the animals multiplied.

The bog disgorged, and huge
Elk put on clothes. Merciless
Hunters pursued the crumbled light.

It had long begun. You
Came late. April, black flags,
Sleds were already on the move.

*Georgia O'Keeffe's*
*"White Rose with Larkspur"*


It says whiteness belongs here
Not just in the puff of upper corners
That it can break rose
In-on-itself to make a nautilus
Or the Host spiral down light for us.
It emits enough to keep blue close
To where greens lie together
Asleep in pale and violet air.

## After Henri Rousseau's "The Dream"

A wall falls from the eye.
The black oboist in the center sees
only us and air.

The moon, an empty plate
above the jungle, waits
to spawn this dream, insensate

With deadmen's fingers,
tulip-eyed buds, two birds,
and monkeys in red gambols.

Nude on the splayed couch
Yadwigha paints the rainbow loincloth
in the jungle's huge embrace.

I meld her with the greenery,
her nipples to the tawny-
maroon corolla's gas fire.

The picture drowns doubt.
In a Parisian orangerie, the redbreast
spurns a haunting elephant.

The black music-maker
billows a spiny flower-cup
to ask who is the dreamer.

# *Treasure*

FOR GARY GOSHGARIAN

True they were always diving for it:
a tramp in the rubbish bucket,
an overheated dog in a puddle rinsing
near where children are playing.

Still, the dull plucky aristocrat
plunges his narrow sack
of antique coin in *la coquette,*
finds the barnacled wreck.

We want the Phoenician toy not
so rotten it melts on touch,
a place to swim down to again
where memory and having are one.

# Samphire

"Halfway down
Hangs one that gathers samphire, dreadful trade."
—*King Lear*


Before the chilling and the vinegar,
the swallowing the healthy oil,
I boil for hours to split
the light green almost algae,
from the bought stalk that survived
drenches of salt and fresh,
where it endured the shale
North Sea wind, and birds.
It rides a thick earth stew—
till, exasperated, I tug it off,
safe.

Unlike the climber who gathered
from a cliff cloven by plants,
whom Edgar imagined for Gloucester,
to feel his blindness on a precipice,
the dangerous remedy in reach.

# *On Looking Into Chapman*

A sick smell
fills him with the dust
of warm nettle.

He stalls at the window.
And feels no rain
or thunder in the left meadow.

He sneezes unfavorably,
as his crammed head settles
on the Greek manual.

Till the evening
starts the field-crickets'
monotonous chirping.

Then the moon stops.
Poised like a coin
in the mouth of a corpse.

Twenty years back, he whines
at a hill near his hometown.
Homer neighs down to climb.

He rises and hums tunes
overheard in early childhood.
Homer paints a cross (a rune)

on his hand. It revives.
Like a spider, it cramps
across the tawny sheaf.

Lusty oil from a lamp
lights, not Troy Wall,
but Hitchin's alder swamp.

His stump of feather roughs
a path to the dark margin.
Like milking, the nib soughs.

Then grayness buries the sharp north sky,
and a cart hobbles the track up the hill.
He reads aloud. His words sound stony and green.
Cadres of critics fall in his fierce eye.

# World of Wine
## Horace, *Odes* I.7

Let others sing of Rhodes or Mytilene,
    Of Ephesos or Corinth's double sea,
The Bacchic walls of Thebes or Delphian
    Apollo, or of Tempe's rough renown.

The whole trick (for some) is to celebrate
    The Virgin's city in perpetual praise
And sport plucked olive branches on the brow.
    Many proclaim, in lays to honor Juno,

Horse-breaking Argos and flashy Mycenae.
    No Spartan odes on discipline for me!
Like rich Larissa, soon those cities dull
    Before Albuna's homey waterfall,

The headstrong Anio, Tibur's grove, and wet
    Full orchards with our restless rivulets.
As often Notus clears the murky heavens
    And does not breed an everlasting rain,

Be wise, my Plancus, remember to mend
    Life's sufferings and sadness with sweet wine,
Where you sit now in camp ablaze with standards
    Or here under thick beech in native Tibur.

When homeless Teucer fled paternal wrath,
    Who failed to right at Troy a brother's life,
Moist with Bacchus, he crowned his brow with poplar,
    Addressed these last as his lagged mates departed:

"Wherever Fortune, kinder than our parent,
    Carry us, allies, friends, we'll be content.
Who can despair with me as seer and leader?
    Apollo promised me triumphant years:

" 'New Salamis makes this superfluous.'
    My best men, often suffering the worst,
Tonight let's muzzle carping care with wine.
    Tomorrow we sail long upon the ocean."

# Viewing Delacroix's Portrait of Chopin

As you move towards him he uncolors
into a map of warring countries:
sea and land one, the face cellular—
the palette has become the picture.

Walk away and intelligence simplifies:
a hooked nose, self-satisfied, theatrical;
driving Beauty away from Beast
with a nibbling at the bones of keys.

So this distance remains categorical:
between ugliness and dissolution;
the light smoking from woman and piano
to scatter music on the darkened wall.

# *Rape*

A brute king in the park,
the broken bottle's truncheon,
his visceral hatreds bled
in the cloistered dark,
average now in Keds
in the next day's thaw.

She is walled in hospital
curtains, learns to draw
his lost face, to warble
with torn tongue, recalls
nightingales still come
undaunted to feed their young.

## Feininger in Houston

Above the manacled light, the glass
and the poured tallness amuse,
like arbitrary trees above the rain forest.

In our shrewd carbolic canyons,
shadow cathedrals reminisce,
regrid the new Euclidean streets.

Beyond Old World, old forest curves,
these granite blocks, these scaffolds
flesh the sun's moonlight.

As after a hammer explodes marble.
Or, unwrapping a cave, a cliff has fallen,
and the monolith is hooded, familiar.

Even friendly.

# Roofing

On a stage above Nantasket beach
My father swung his golden hammer,
Declared himself in singing strokes
Neptune in a tarnished Irish suit.

Instinctive as a crow his shadow
Rode the ocean's raise and shunt.
Crossed the sand and powdered wall,
Past the white Victorian town.

When cigarette smoke gathered to cloud,
He nodded, and I shouldered up the bale,
Tarry and flapping, like a great black cod,
Where each nail, each new tile jelled.

FRANCIS BLESSINGTON brings to his writing an understanding of his native New England—especially in his sensitive perceptions of nature—and his experiences as a traveller, reinforced by a background in classical literature. Although this is his first book of poems, his work has been widely published in magazines and periodicals. In a different but complementary vein are his other books: *Paradise Lost and the Classical Epic*, 1979, and *Paradise Lost: Ideal and Tragic Epic* (to be published next year). With Guy Rotella, he has edited *The Motive for Metaphor: Essays on Modern Poetry in Honor of Samuel French Morse*. Born in Boston, he was educated at Boston College, Northeastern University, and Brown. He presently teaches at Northeastern and lives with his wife and his young son and daughter in Woburn, Massachusetts.

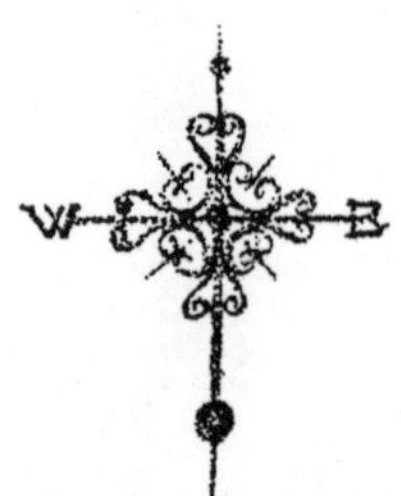

This book was typeset in Linotron Sabon with
headings in Perpetua by TCI, Chicopee, Massachusetts,
printed at the Cabinet Press, Inc., Milford, New Hampshire,
and bound at the New Hampshire Bindery, Concord.